Siberian Tiger

The World's Biggest Cat

by Meish Goldish

Consultant: Andrea Heydlauff
Managing Director, Panthera

BEARPORT
PUBLISHING

New York, New York

Credits

Cover, © Dennis Donohue/Shutterstock; TOC, © Dennis Donohue/Shutterstock; 4, Kathrin Ayer; 4-5, © Wildlife/Peter Arnold Inc.; 6L, © Wildlife/Peter Arnold Inc.; 6R, © Konrad Wothe/Minden Pictures; 7, © Goran Cakmazovic/Shutterstock; 8, © age fotostock/SuperStock; 9, © A. & J. Visage/Peter Arnold; 10, © Tom & Pat Leeson/Ardea; 11, © Tom Brakefield/Corbis; 12, © Keren Su/Getty Images; 13, © Chuck Pefley/Alamy; 14T, © David Chapman/Alamy; 14B, © Niall Benvie/Nature Picture Library; 15, © Toshiji Fukuda/Nature Production/Minden Pictures; 16, © imagebroker/Alamy; 17, © David Moir/Reuters/Landov; 18, © blickwinkel/Alamy; 19, © Tom and Pat Leeson; 21, © Wildlife/Peter Arnold Inc.; 22L, © Leksele/Shutterstock; 22C, © Stephen Meese/iStockphoto; 22R, © blickwinkel/Alamy; 23TL, © Tom & Pat Leeson/Ardea; 23TR, © Petr Mašek/Shutterstock; 23BL, © Eric Gevaert/Shutterstock; 23BR, © Toshiji Fukuda/Nature Production/Minden Pictures; 23BKG, © Ewan Chesser/Shutterstock.

Publisher: Kenn Goin
Editorial Director: Adam Siegel
Creative Director: Spencer Brinker
Design: Otto Carbajal
Photo Researcher: Michael Fergenson

Library of Congress Cataloging-in-Publication Data

Goldish, Meish.
  Siberian tiger : the world's biggest cat / by Meish Goldish.
      p. cm. — (More supersized!)
  Includes bibliographical references and index.
  ISBN-13: 978-1-936087-28-0 (library binding)
  ISBN-10: 1-936087-28-6 (library binding)
  1. Tigers—Juvenile literature. I. Title.
  QL737.C23G64 2010
  599.756—dc22
                                    2009038239

For more information, write to Bearport Publishing Company, Inc., 101 Fifth Avenue, Suite 6R, New York, New York 10003. Printed in the United States of America in North Mankato, Minnesota.

112009
090309CGC

10 9 8 7 6 5 4 3 2 1

Contents

Long and Heavy

The Siberian tiger is the biggest cat in the world.

A Siberian tiger is almost as long as two motor scooters.

A male Siberian tiger can grow up to be 11 feet (3.3 m) long. It can weigh more than 455 pounds (206 kg). Males are larger than females.

Snowy Homes

Siberian tigers live in very cold parts of Russia and China.

They roam through the forests there.

Deep snow often covers the ground, but that doesn't stop these big cats from getting around.

Their large **paws** act like snowshoes, which keep the tigers from sinking into the snow.

paws

Siberian Tigers in the Wild

Where Siberian tigers live

Russia

Mongolia

China

North Korea

South Korea

Japan

Pacific Ocean

Siberian tigers once lived in Siberia, a large area of land in central and eastern Russia, as well as in Northeast China. Today, Siberian tigers are also called Amur tigers because they now mainly live in the cold Amur regions of the Russian Far East.

7

Keeping Warm

The temperature is often below freezing in the places where Siberian tigers live.

Cold weather is no problem for the big cats, however.

Their bodies are covered with thick, long fur, which keeps them warm.

During the winter, a tiger's coat grows thicker and longer to keep the animal extra-warm.

Living Alone

Adult Siberian tigers live far apart from one another.

Each animal needs its own area of land that is big enough for it to find enough food to eat.

In the woods, tigers scratch the trees with their sharp, curved **claws**.

The scratches tell other tigers, "Keep out of my space!"

claws

A male tiger may claim up to 772 square miles (2,000 sq km) of land for itself. A female may claim up to 174 square miles (451 sq km).

Finding Food

Siberian tigers are powerful hunters.

They roam the woods looking for large animals to eat.

Even though they search mostly at night, they are still able to find their **prey**.

Like all tigers, they see very well in the dark.

They also have very good hearing.

In the dark, Siberian tigers see five times better than people.

Quiet Killers

Sika and red deer as well as wild boars are some of the large animals that Siberian tigers hunt.

The big cat quietly sneaks up on its prey.

Then it leaps on the animal and sinks its sharp teeth into the prey's neck.

The tiger drags the dead animal to a hiding place and begins to eat.

Once it is full, the tiger may not eat again for several days.

sika deer

wild boar

After killing a big animal, a Siberian tiger may eat up to 77 pounds (35 kg) of meat in one night. It then hides the rest of the food for later.

Tiger Cubs

A female Siberian tiger usually has one to four baby tigers, or **cubs**, at a time.

They are usually born in summer or fall.

The mother feeds her cubs milk from her body for the first two months of their lives.

After the cubs are two months old, their mother starts bringing them meat to eat.

cub

On Their Own

Mother tigers teach their cubs how to hunt.

The young tigers are quick learners.

By the time they are one and a half years old, they can hunt for food on their own.

By age three or four, the tigers are ready to leave their mother and live by themselves.

Each tiger can now start its own family of big cats.

A baby Siberian tiger weighs only about 3 pounds (1.4 kg) when it is born. In just two years, it can weigh as much as 250 pounds (113 kg)!

Tigers in Danger

Because Siberian tigers are so powerful, other animals do not hunt them.

People are their only enemy.

They hunt the tigers for their fur, meat, and bones.

Only about 400 Siberian tigers are now left in the wild.

Today, there are laws against hunting them.

People are working hard to make sure the giant cats are able to live safely in their cold, snowy homes for many years to come.

Siberian tigers are also in danger because the forests where they live are being destroyed. Some people cut down the trees so that they can sell the wood.

More Big Cats

Siberian tigers are members of the cat family, which also includes lions, leopards, and jaguars. All cats are part of a larger group of animals called mammals. Almost all mammals give birth to live young instead of laying eggs. The babies drink milk from their mothers. Mammals are also warm-blooded and have hair or fur on their skin.

Here are three more big cats.

Lion

The lion is the second-largest cat. It can grow up to 8.5 feet (2.6 m) long.

Jaguar

The jaguar is the third-largest cat. It can grow up to 7 feet (2.1 m) long.

Snow Leopard

The snow leopard can grow up to 6.5 feet (1.9 m) long.

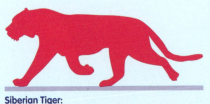

Siberian Tiger:
11 feet/3.3 m

Lion:
8.5 feet/2.6 m

Jaguar:
7 feet/2.1 m

Snow Leopard:
6.5 feet/1.9 m

Glossary

claws (KLAWZ)
hard, sharp nails on the ends of the fingers or toes of an animal

paws (PAWZ)
the feet of an animal that has four feet and claws

cubs (KUHBZ)
baby tigers

prey (PRAY)
an animal that is hunted by another animal for food

Index

Read More

Cooper, Jason. *Siberian Tiger.* Vero Beach, FL: Rourke (1997).

St. Pierre, Stephanie. *Siberian Tigers (In the Wild).* Chicago: Heinemann (2001).

Thomson, Sarah L. *Amazing Tigers!* New York: HarperCollins (2004).

Learn More Online

To learn more about Siberian tigers, visit
www.bearportpublishing.com/MoreSuperSized